RASTAFARI
Lavi Ayisyen

PUBLISHED BY:
SOLOMON & MAKEDA PUBLISHING

Rastafari

Lavi

Ayisyen

Written by: Ras Go Go

Copyright © 2016 by Solomon & Makeda Publishing

All Rights Reserved. No parts of this book may be reproduced in any form without the express written consent of Publisher/Authors, except in the case of brief quotations embodied within relevant articles and book reviews for print and electronic media.

The Dissonant's Slave

Quick to run and do what he say,

You are the dissonant's slave.

If you harm one of your black sisters or brothers,

You are the dissonant's slave.

Calling beautiful black queens bitches and hoes,

You are the dissonant's slave.

Not caring for your sons and daughters,

You are the dissent's slave.

Not listening to your spiritual, and physical Mother &

Father, You are the dissonant's slave.

Refusing to assist in the rise of the beautiful Black African

Nation, You are the dissonant's slave.

Looking at our black sisters and brothers in Africa

Different from yourself,

You are the dissonant's slave.

Promoting separatism amongst people of color,

You are the dissonant's slave.

Destroying one another and stagnating the advancement

of our people,

You are the dissonant's slave.

Start coalescing and stop being the dissonant's slave by

Loving thyself and thy people,
You are not the dissonant's slave!!

****

Anointing my crown to keep my mind & thoughts in a righteous & pure state. Anointing my feet every day, so that my path may be
cleared of any snare that is before me is providence. Anointing, on daily journey, is for keeping spiritual wickedness in high places in check, and, away from breaching or intruding on the
sanctums, mind, body, and atman.
To be sanctified with prayer oil is providence and
Spiritual protection for InI and InI loved ones.
The sanctity of prayer oil is causing the wicked ones to
Reveal themselves in abominable ways.
InI and the two wendem anoint everyday as we trod the Belly of the Beast, and, coalesce as the trinity in the way of life. Paying homage to the atman with prayer oil and incense in introspection.

****

All, things in this universe know that they are a part of the Most High's Oneness, and therefore give their praises and Performs rituals all the time.

Even nature performs its rituals of oneness, the great Rock standing still, Is being obedient to displaying its power. The great waters gives life and washes away all impurities, and does the wave dance. The great trees, including the Tree of Life, give shade and feeds knowledge of good and corrects evil. The wind blowing is a ritual.
Awaking from sleep is a ritual.
Thinking is also a ritual.
The soil and the yielding of its fruits is performing a ritual.
Walking is a ritual, etc.

****

The cyber world and the technology is poisoning the minds & atman of the children and world with pollution and non-attunement with there atman. This way of life is not in alignment with the natural way of life, this causes families to not have the proper relationships. We need to realign and be obedient to the Universal Law with power in place and in order; with the Supreme Universal Self. Not cybernetics or devices and the vice that they upload into our atman. Let's start observing everything with Subtle Spectacles. All of nature, like the sun, moon, and stars are being obedient and are in alignment with Divine Universal Law.

****

Thoughts are like a marathon; the mind will run a marathon if you let it. Control your thoughts and mind by passing the baton in the race of positive vibrations. What emotion controls your decision on what's right & wrong, positive or negative, and where do they come from within you? Do your desire come from a place of love?

A place where Supreme Love dwells is where our feelings for what is right or wrong comes from. The thoughts create the emotion that create the feelings which causes the vibrations of positive and negative.

Observe your thoughts and feed them with food from the divine. The observer needs to feel the mind in its essences, Good Positive Vibrations.

A mind with G. P. V. seeds or Divine Food will not and does not harvest anything that's not divine.

Physics says that energy cannot be created or destroyed, but it can be converted. So let us convert this energy that's within everything and everyone, so that the Supreme Universal

Self can be realized.

Aquarius, give life to all the other ages as well as the

Stardust called life.

Ras Jah GoGo

The Ulotrichous'sPrayer

I love thee O'thy darkness,

O'thy voidness, and thy blackness.

Let InI give thanks and praise to thy one true self within,

there is beauty and goodness in melanin.

Grateful, Faithful, and Truthful is its color in thy sight.

O'thy beginning of all vibrant colors, let the Star of Africa

shine within. Rise O'thy origin of man's heart

ulotrichous's, be

proud O' beautiful ulotrichous one.

Maven in coalescing with the inner rainbow of love and

life. O'thou of great valor and rectitude, let the

introspection that is needed be given to InI by the strong

arm of providence.

O'thy darkness, and voidness let Jah Black-Light come

and continue to shine in InI forever more Amen.

Ras Jah GoGo

Perception of A Mom

Mirror mimics, beautiful to display the unique
For it shows what lies Beneath, for Diamond Girl.
Curved just right; glare within
the darkest night. She knows what it takes to expand the
brand of Diamond Girl.
It takes that stain of coal, the
temperature of Mars, the time of
a Goddess, and the grace of unity,
for Diamond Girl.
Overtime, glamour multiples, Look up
Look Down, they're rubies, they're pearls,
they're crystals and gem stones, gold to
support those all for Diamond Girl.
Remember jewels are passed down,
So if she plucked you, show off yourself
to everyone downtown, but let them know
you came from uptown, from a Diamond Angel.

Your Son,
by: Douglas Jean

Perception of A Wombman

It is with the highest appreciation that I present myself, in Spirit, to those who are gathered together in order to celebrate the Elevation of an Angel. My Angel was brought here in February of 1978 eleven months after I arrived in March of 1977. Causing us both to be born under the sign of Pisces; a match We physically met in the seventh grade, and all I could see was her beauty, her light. She proved to be smart, caring, and spiritual, and she affected me in the most profound ways. When our Son was born, little did I know that her shear will would make him my own role model. In fact, all of our kids bare markings of her unimaginable Love that she has for them, it's in the Love that they themselves have for each other. They are manifestation of her Spirit being caring, smart, and Spiritual. To know her is to adore her. Her friendship is not part-time or temporary. What she gives you is a gift for life. Through troubling times or times of joy you knew that you had her support & comfort. She is the true definition of a wife, that's a fact. For me, no one can truly take her place, and they won't be able to, because she will always be here in spirit. It's that spirit that's eternal, and there is where she has her peace, so will we all. I thank you all for attending this celebration of Life. May the peace of God expand within Us all.

Ras Jah GoGo

Words of His Imperial Majesty Haile Selassie I

"BUT THESE, TOO, AS WERE THE PHRASES OF THE COVENANT ARE ONLY WORDS; THEIR VALUE DEPENDS WHOLLY ON OUR WILL TO OBSERVE AND HONOR THEM AND GIVE THEM CONTENT AND MEANING."

Words, power, and sound used to produce and effect for a purpose it is said that a prayer a day will keep the devil away. The words in the prayer are said then the sounds of those words are heard, and then the words and sound activate the power which keeps the devil behind thee. Words have the power that travels in sound waves and influence the universe and ether. That's why observing and honoring them in their fullness and highest regards are necessary. Because as it is said so shall it be, and as mankind say it with conviction and intent it shall manifest. So, that's why words can be used to hurt others and yourself, I know that one should be aware of what is said and when it is said. And there's a power that exist in what is uttered which can influence creation and everything that exist in it.
Genesis 1:3; Mark 4:39-41; and Joshua 1:8

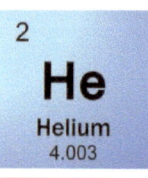

Words of Toussaint-Louverture

"IN OVER THROWING ME, YOU HAVE CUT DOWN ONLY THE TRUCK OF THE TREE OF LIBERTY IN SAINT DOMINQUE. IT WILL SPRING UP AGAIN BY THE ROOTS FOR THEY ARE NUMEROUS AND DEEP".

The over throwing that is being mentioned is of and comes from the oppressors who are in war mode constantly. Trees are liberated by nature, but in this context it is for the liberty of a people that represent the trees being oppressed. Manifold are the people of color who will rise back up to claim their royal position, in a world of oppression. The truth is always in the roots of a thing, we need to get back to that and explore our culture, heritage, way of life, and absorb and fertilize our generations of Black Kings and Queens. Our ancestors blood and tears shall not be in vain, prosper we shall, but remember before we sow our seeds we must know our roots. The seeds are planted and the roots are formed then the tree produces and bring forth its fruits. The tree and the roots are numerous in their dimension. The tree has branches and leaves which can represent different states of minds or different journeys, truths, and paths in life. And deep are our values in mind, body, and soul.

Words of The Honorable Minister Louis Farrakhan

"WE WANT A GREAT PEOPLE AND STRONG PEOPLE AND IF IT MEANS THAT WE HAVE TO TAKE THE HANDS OF THOSE WHO OPPOSE OUR RIGHTEOUS LIFE FOR OUR PEOPLE THEN WE ARE READY TO GO TO WAR NOW."

Every nation has its want or need to be a great people. But the want for our people comes from being deprived of the opportunity to be a great people, that we once were. Strong is our genetic makeup, we are strong in mind, body, and spirit and in numerous other aspects. A righteous way of life has and always will be a means for us to strive as a people, for it is our purpose in life. When we are in alignment with our supreme universal Self then we will be the mighty people and the greatest people. Let us take into consideration any physical, mental, and spiritual pollutions in our path; we will cleanse it out of our destiny.

Words of Public Enemy

"FIGHT THE POWER!"

There are many different front's this fight can be addressed on. We have fights against Racial Discrimination, Social Economics, The Spiritual and Educational. Fights against Governments and other Nations. And of course, we have the Powers That Be the Government, Military, and Religion. Also, the many of weapons of Mass Destruction, Atomic and Nuclear. It is also important that the people should know what it is that they are fighting against, and that the Power is within them. So they can fight for what's right. Haile Selassie 1 is the Power of the Trinity, the Power is within. Education is power, Silence is power, the Mind is power, Thoughts are power. The Power is in the people, and the People is the power. The fight is within ourselves, against the System of oppression and against any and everything that is in a
ungodly state. The fight is physically, mentally, and spiritually, it's against one another, and the universe. It's a fight of good over evil, the pure and impure, holy and the unholy. Ephesians 6:12

Words of Malcom X

"BY ANY MEANS NECESSARY"

We as a people of color have many means that needs to be addressed. First, we need to keep in mind our purpose, which is of great importance, and we need a sense of direction. We need to educate ourselves, provide for ourselves, believe in ourselves, and love ourselves. These are some of what I think are necessary for us as a people, we must uplift our mighty race by means of physicality, mentality, and spirituality. Then every other necessity will be met. I'm talking financial, economics, and education etc.

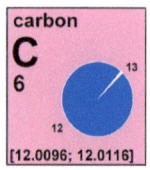

Words of The Honorable Minister Louis Farrakhan

"YOU HAVE NO UNITY, YOU DON'T SEE THAT. YOUR UNITY IS YOUR KEY TO YOUR SUCCESS, BECAUSE YOU ARE DIVIDED, SO DISUNITED SO FULL OF PETTY ENVY AND JEALOUSY YOU DON'T SEE YOUR UNITY IS THE KEY TO YOUR SUCCESS."

Because the Most High has made everything in the universe to co-exist. So, Africans need to unite as a people and a race before they can coalesce with other races. Unite your body, your mind, and your spirit. We should also unite our resources in education, finances, and invest in ourselves; so that success is obtained. Unity is an unstoppable force! We were divided into sections and distributed to different parts of the world. This separation has perpetuated and now has become apart of our behaviors and way of life. Subtle feelings of jealousy are involved; therefore, we are not able to recognize the success of our fellow African brother. Petty envy, jealously, and being disunited will all dissipate the flow of unity.

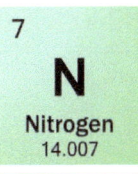

Words of the Honorable Marcus Garvey

"ONE LOVE, ONE AIM, ONE DESTINY!"

Love is the only solution that can save a wretched nation of oppressors and ungodly bigots. Love is a very powerful feeling and experience; which leads to peace in all aspects conceivable, love creates life. Love is an interchangeable feeling, it was in the darkness of the womb. Love is all we need to propel life and humanly. Our aim should be a course that is direct and full of purpose, intended to fulfil prophecy with providence. Destiney is a promise we shall transcend. One God! One Jah! One Allah! One Yahweh? Whatever one may call their Atman our universal goal is to be reunited with that essence of Oneness. Holy Quran 2:136

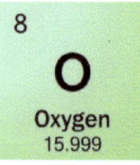

Words of The Most Honorable Elijah Muhammad

"WE ARE THE ROOT OF MATHEMATICS. GOD HIMSELF IS UNIT NO. **1**."

There's a divine and mutual interrelation between the root and God, the Alpha and Omega. Everything that exist has a mathematical expression, which is God. Therefore, God Himself is Unit No.1., uniting us in a harmonious way and giving us providence. Nothing is always Something. From zero we become One with God Himself, the Divine One, two, and the Trinity. Genesis 1:2-3

Words of The Most Honorable Elijah Muhammad

"ABOVE ALL MAN'S HABITS PEACE IS THE MOST SATISFYING OF HIS LIFE."

The above quote that's being used are referring to as a standard, a high rank or degree; which a comparison can be made to His Imperial Majesty Haile Selassie 1. Known as The Prince of Peace, so peace is above love and joy when aspects of emotions are entertained. The state of peace is tranquility, and should be observed above all of man's habits; and is a tool that is used to keep thoughts and emotions in check, and in harmony with man's inner self. When mankind subdues their carnal and fleshly desires and become immersed in their Atman, then we will be able to coalesce the Trinity of love, joy, peace, and these will give us substance that; will sustain us on our life's journey. What is life? Some would say it is to live or subsist oneself, and that it is vital, being the existence of an individual. It is also said to be the state of being animated. But what The Most Honorable Elijah Muhammad is saying is, man's Way of Life is satisfying when peace is obtained.

Words of The Most Honorable Elijah Muhammad

"EVERYTHING WRITTEN IN THE BIBLE IS WRITTEN TO GIVE US A PICTURE OF WHAT IS HAPPENING TODAY".

Everything that is written in the Bible is Truth, because we have evidence of them, and we see them happening today. Every day of our life the writings gives us vivid pictures and instructions, with providence for the future. The signs and the times are clearly revelations of what was written in the Holy Scriptures. There are wars against other nations. Mankind killing mankind. We have division in religions; homosexuality is as it was written about in Sodom. We have natural disasters, such as floods, earthquakes, and we also have false preachers and teachers, etc. Holy Quran 7:95

Words of The Most Honorable Elijah Muhammad

"REAR YOU CHILDREN UP IN THE WORD OF ALLAH. ALLAH SAYS, TEACH THEM OF ME. BURN IT INTO THEIR HEARTS."

"We have a duty as parents, to raise our children upright. Allah has given to us instructions to teach them by bringing up. The burn that is being spoken of is to refine their hearts, minds, and bodies. The foundation for spiritual enlightenment is in the Word of The One Allah it is the best food that will nourish. It is good to eat an abundance of the Word. You should also cherish the Words of the Most High and wrap them around your hearts, forevermore."

Words of Ras-go-go

"THE HANDS OF THE ALMIGHTY YAH RASTAFARI ARE INFINITELY ON OUR SIDE."
ROMANS
8:31

"When the Hands of the Divine clock is in our favor, and every step is calculated towards our divine purpose, then being reunited with our essence shall cause prophecy to be fulfilled, in a divine way and at a divine time. For the creator has the whole universe in His Hands. We will not be afraid or conquered by illusion or confusion of any kind. God is all we will ever need and going to need. He has always been there, and will always be; so give Thanks & Praises for the Hands of the Almighty Yah Rastafari perpetually."

Words of The Most Honorable Elijah Muhammad

"THE LIGHT OF GOD IS THE LIGHT OF THE HEREAFTER WHICH WILL GUIDE THE PEOPLE LIKE THE LIGHT OF THE SUN."

"Man and woman must coalesce in the divine Light within them; so that they can cultivate, illuminate, and then elevate to and through the divine spheres. Physically we are incarcerated, but mentally and spiritually we are liberated. The Light! The Light! O' how beautiful it is; it gives life to the people living in darkness. Please O' Light, shine your everlasting Light on us, so that the people may find their way to what is delightful. The light is getting brighter, because we have gotten closer to what's right love and light, with Jah to shield us from wrong."

14
Si
Silicon
28.086

Words of Ras-go-go

"The Red, Gold, and Green are of stupendous beauty, virtue, and values to the world."

"The Glory of God is evidently Pure, Divine, and full of Grace, The Red is the great vibrant energy that exist in all of creation. It is eminent as the luminous sun, Big Red. Gold is divine beauty extracted from the Glory of God, for this reason everything is made to shine, because He has blessed us with pure splendor. He has given us a standard to be measured by. The grace of the Green Tree of Life is available to all, so that we may flourish in the spiritual and material way of life, on a scale based on truth, righteousness, and equality for all colors."

Words of The Most Honorable Elijah Muhammad

"DON'T BE CAREFUL THAT YOU AGREE ON RIGHT BUT, BE CAREFUL THAT YOU DON'T AGREE ON WRONG."

"What I think is being expressed in the message above is, right is right and wrong is wrong, and should be observed for what it is through trial and error. One will be lead to what is of truth and right, but be aware you don't amiss. It is easy to agree on doing wrong, where as it is difficult to do right. Therefore, one needs to be aware of what it is that he/she is coming in to terms with when dealing with wrong."

Words of The Most Honorable Elijah Muhammad

"YOUR CHILDREN HAVE TO BE PREPARED FOR A FUTURE THEY HAVE NOT LIVED. YOU MUST SHAPE YOUR CHILD."

"What is being said, by the Most Honorable Elijah Muhammad, is that we as parents must understand what our position is in life; which is to give our children a fair chance at the future, by accumulating and cultivating the proper resources. We need to give them the education, religion, and finances. Our culture, heritage, and history should be what we use to mold them. A new beginning and age is at hand. For the providence of our generations, we need to learn and teach them everything, so that our children are ready for whatever, whenever, forever."

Words by Ras-go-go

"Providence is power and purpose; for the elevation of our coloured nations."

"To be cared for and given direction by God is our birthright. We just need to take heed and be obedient to all aspects of his teachings and revelations; by total devotion and admiration. All our life we have been given the power and ability of Clairvoyance, So that we are able to emulate the Most High for the highest enlightening of the divine love, joy, and peace."

Words of Ras-go-go

"Enounce the enmity with the red, white, and the blue, because the Red, Gold, and Green is coming through full of the truth."

"What I'm saying is you're either with us or against us, so pick a side. We are no longer going to deal with the ungodly and follies of what your colors stand for. So, we no longer pledge to something that was never meant for our people or the progress of our nations and humanity. The Red, Gold, and Green, only seeks One love, One aim, One destiny for all of mankind."

Words of Ras-go-go

"Coloured nations providences is a blessing for a purpose to spiritually elevate and mentally emancipate."

"My interpretation of this is that to adhere to the power of providence is a great importance to our people, and to those who are misled by an ungodly way of life. Because providence is pure care and divine guidance from the creator Himself, it is an unlimited source of mercy, grace, and love; the blessing and purpose that's obtain through being obedient to the beckoning of the subtle voice within. This will provide liberty of the highest form from all wicked entanglements, and will enable one to fulfill their destiny."

Words of His Imperial Majesty Haile Selassie I

"FROM AMERICANS WHO SHARE OUR DESIRES AND WHO ARE WILLING TO COOPERATE WITH US, WE SEEK THAT SELF-SUFFICIENCY WHICH WILL ENABLE US TO PLAY OUR RIGHTFUL ROLE IN INTERNATIONAL AFFAIRS & LIVE IN FULL HARMONY WITH ALL MEN"

"Racial discrimination must be and will be eradicated, so that mankind may live in Itopia. Righteousness is our weapon of choice, it will be needed from all nations, and with that we will prevail. Our rightful role in this case, I think, mean that our affairs should be embedded in and surrounded, in regard to humanity on a large scale, a universal one. We must engage in a spiritual and mystical love thyself type of way of life; before we can love our neighboring nations and regions in the world as one human race. We need to have a positive vibration that will bring about a complete way of life, for all of mankind."

21
Sc
Scandium
44.956

Words of The Honorable Minister Louis Farrakhan

"AS MY BROTHER, WHAT IS HE SAYING? HE'S TELLING BLACK KIDS TO GET A GOOD EDUCATION, HE'S TELLING BLACK KIDS TO LEARN THE KNOWLEDGE OF THEMSELVES, SO THEY CAN LOVE THEMSELVES."

"What The Honorable Minister Louis Farrakhan is saying is that he has so much love for us, and as our elder and teacher he's giving to us the advice that is much needed. We need to apply ourselves by educating ourselves, because education is power and key to our success. And the Minister understands that, so we as a people must invest in a good education for the future of our kids. Brothers and sisters, we are required to learn, unlearn, and relearn, and propel in gaining knowledge about our ancestors, and everything that exist, so that we may experience the love of ourselves."

Words of Martin Luther King Jr.

"SO I'M HAPPY TONIGHT., I'M NOT WORRIED ABOUT ANYTHING. I'M NOT FEARING ANY MAN."

"When we trust in God Almighty we will be filled with joy. We will overcome fear, and will not have a care in the world. We will be firmly rooted in Him. We as a people must not fret, for there will be threats made against our life to derail our mission at hand. Dr. King is letting us know that, no matter what, we must stay on the course; so that we may achieve our goals in obtaining equality, justice, and liberty for all mankind."

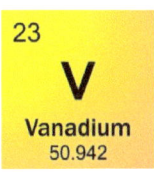

Words of Martin Luther King Jr.

"Mine eyes had seen the glory of the coming of the Lord."

"Righteous we must be, before we can see the coming of our Lord and His glory. Our hearts must be clean and our minds must be pure, then can we observe and honor the glory of God in an elevated spiritual and mystical way."

Words of Unknown

"Black is beautiful when it realizes itself and becomes itself"

"Just being who you are is a beautiful thing in itself; whether you are black, white, red, or brown people. Who, in general, need to first know themselves. Black people need to journey back to the Mother Land, Africa. It's the origin of beauty, love, and peace. We must explore our culture, heritage, and history; then we will be able to experience the beautiful blackness in ourselves. It is truly beautiful."

Words of Unknown

"AFRICAN-AMERICANS SHOULD CONTROL THEIR RESOURCES, THEIR COMMUNITY AND THE PRODUCTS OF THEIR HANDS AND MINDS."

"Owning our own businesses, schools, and banks are productive tools that can be used for the advancement of our people. African-Americans and the ideas of their minds have shaped many civilizations. We are creative and skillful with our hands, so with our hands and our minds we can build a nation within a nation. For instance, Physical Power! Mental Power! And Spiritual Power! Are and should be some of our main interest, because these components are essential for the development of our men, women, and children and our future."

Words of Malcom X

"Africans in Africa and Africans in America need to know that they were inextricable bound together and would rise and fall together."

"We must coalesce! It is necessary that we stand firm and convicted in the midst of it all. Success and failure goes hand in hand. The suffrage that the Africans in Africa and the Africans in America are facing are one in the same. It will bring about the same results, inspiration, and elevation."

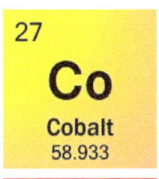

Words of James Brown

" Say It Loud, I'm Black and I'm Proud"

"Don't be ashamed of who or what you are; black, red, or white. Be proud and believe in who and what you are. Knowing thyself and Accepting thyself will lead you to loving thyself no matter what. So, repeat after me, I am that I am and I am Proud of it."

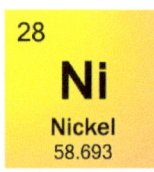

Words of Aretha Franklin

"R–E–S–P–E–C–T"

"I respect and Love the God in you and everything that exist. RESPECT is due to all of mankind, but we need to first RESPECT ourselves. Then we will be able to RESPECT others, and all of God's creations."

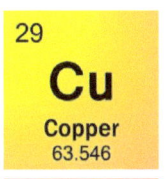

Words of Marvin Gaye

"Whʌt's Going On?"

Good question, and here's my answer. We have an oppressive system and racial genocide, and war on the mind, spirit, and body. We cannot forget, of course, the hypocrisies, and injustices going on in the world."

30 Zn Zinc 65.39

Poem

Your mind is pure and your heart is clean, you're the virtuous woman of my dream. By the side of every strong and righteous man you cling, but what will it take to find you. You're one of a kind, but I will know when I have found you, because your lights are so bright. And on any given night, I will single you out amongst the not so bright. How is it that you lay so innocently neat on the universe fabric sheet and not cheat with any of the stars and cosmic freaks.

Words of Ras-go-go

"Perception is everything, and I perceive the red, the white, and the blue to be all the above."

"The red you are dreadful! The blue you are not true to anyone but you. The white all you want to do is fight everyone and everything that's right."
"The red is morally dead! The white will like and cause strife, because it is not right and it has no light. And the blue how not true are you to anyone but you."

"The red y'all know that, y'all always morally dead and dreadful, the white yeah right, ya'll ain't never gonna do right, but y'all gonna start some wars and cause strife. And the blue, what you gonna do when God comes for you, for not being true."

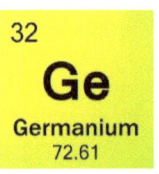

Words of Ras-go-go

"WORDS ARE THE TOOLS OF THINKING."

"People use words to relate to one another. Words are also used to communicate your feelings and thoughts to them, influence them, persuade them, and control them. Through words you shape your own destiny, that's what I believe and know. For example: the righteous words that preceded out of the mouth of the great Bob Marley, One Love can unite all of humanity. Words and phrases are packed with C-4. A single word can destroy a friendship, can start or end wars. Words can and will change the direction of our life."

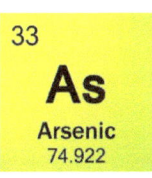

Words of Frederick Douglass

"PEACE BETWEEN RACES IS NOT TO BE SECURED BY DEGRADING ONE RACE AND EXALTING ANOTHER; BY GIVING POWER TO ONE RACE AND WITHHOLDING IT FROM ANOTHER; BUT BY MAINTAINING A STATE OF EQUAL JUSTICE BETWEEN ALL CLASSES. FIRST PURE, THEN PEACEABLE."

"When a race of people are being deprived and denied the necessities of financial, terrestrial, economical, and psychological ways of life, by all means, this is a form of war. That's why when two entities are engaged in war, at some point, the so-called rules become nullified. For example: in the city of Miami, let's say there are two groups that are beefing for whatever reason, and one decides to poison the other's water supply, that everyone in the city drinks from, including kids, that would be a major violation. That's why I think that there's no rules to war. War has no rules when a certain race is being targeted and a certain mechanism is being applied. I am talking financially, terrestrially, economically and psychologically. I did not mention physically or spiritually, because for the first four hundred years our race have endured those two aspects."

Words of His Imperial Majesty

Haile Selassie I

"On the question of racial discrimination, the Addis Ababa Conference taught, to those who will learn, this further lesson: That until the philosophy which holds one race superior and another inferior is finally and permanently discredited and abandoned: That until there are no longer first-class and second class citizens of any nation; That until the color of a man's skin is of no more significance than the color of his eyes; That until the basic human rights are equally guaranteed to all without regard to race; That until that day, the dream of lasting peace and world citizenship and the rule of international morality will remain but a fleeting illusion, to be pursued but never attained; And until the ignoble and unhappy regimes that hold our brothers in Angola, in Mozambique and in South Africa in subhuman bondage have been toppled and destroyed; until bigotry and prejudice and malicious and inhuman self-interest have been replaced by understanding and tolerance and good-will; Until all Africans stand and speak as free beings, equal in the eyes of all men, as they are in the eyes of Heaven; Until that day, the African continent will not know peace. We Africans will fight, if necessary, and we know that we shall win, as we are confident in the victory of good over evil."

"The Power of the Trinity Haile Selassie I has blown The Divine Trumpet and it should have been heard by those who have divine ears to hear it, and should have caused those who hear the mystical sound of it to take heed, and engage and propel towards the occasion at hand. It will lead us in fulfilling our elevation as a Beautiful Black Race, because we, The Conquering Lions of Judah, shall sunder these chains of injustice and inhumanity; of police brutality, racism, and imprisonment of our brothers from out of the belly of the beast. Not just physically, but spiritually and mystically. There's a confederacy and bureaucracy in place to keep our Black Beautiful Africans abroad in a machination and erroneous captive states. The only thing we as kinsman want is for all of humanity to coalesce and not degenerate. And we are persistent in our pursuit for liberty and equality for all of mankind, and for one common divine goal of Holy Oneness in Ithiopia, with Utopia for all."

Words of Langston Hughes

"O, LET AMERICA BE AMERICA—
THE LAND THAT NEVER HAS BEEN YET—
AND YET. MUST BE – THE LAND WHERE EVERYMAN
IS FREE. THE LAND THAT'S MINE – THE POOR
MAN'S, INDIAN'S, NEGRO'S, ME – WHO MADE
AMERICA. WHOSE SWEAT. AND BLOOD, WHOSE
FAITH AND PAIN... MUST BRING BACK OUR MIGHTY
DREAM AGAIN."

"I would with a righteous and positive motive make announcement, and then engage peacefully, demonstrating my intentions with various mechanism that would involve writings, advertisement, and propaganda of the unlawful acts that where committed. I would also opprobrium the confederacy and bureaucracy of the corrupt government. A government such as the U.S. has operated with licentious and erroneous ideology, and is considered a behemoth of a nation to me. It should be recognized for its machination of cruelty, injustice, and bigotry against other nations and people of color. And because of their lunacy, they are committing suicide without understanding. My will to exist is justifying their

existence through providence, and the moment I-n-I eximious they will exist no more. The extreme folly and character disorders they possess prevents them from the mental capacity required to be righteous and lawful; when dealing in civil, criminal or human relations and responsibility. And because of their unsoundness, they cannot be trusted, and must be exposed and opposed or else we will be under some laicism; which I'm not for but I'm for laissez-faire."

Rastafari Lavi Ayisyen

"Haiti's rich cultural treasures are an appropriate extension of its history as one of the most influential nations in the world, particularly among people of African descent. It's legacy as the first country in which Africans were able to overthrow the system of race-based slavery remains a source of pride, and Haitians are optimistic about a more prosperous future that will fittingly reflect their remarkable past..."

"Genocide is the deliberate and systematic mistreatment or extermination of an entire people, and is the most extreme of racial hatred. Genocide is practiced and was practiced by Europeans against African people in Africa, America, and Abroad."

Different Types of Racism

"Institutional racism is policies that restrict the opportunities of minorities in communities, schools, and business. Institutional racism is intentional and produce harmful results. For example, institutional racism is the use of racial profiling in law enforcement. Racial profiling is the practice of using skin color as a basis for pulling over black citizens in police encounters, like a traffic stop.

"Another example of Institutional racism is when a company may not hire you because you are ulotrichous's that company policy would limit the opportunities available to blacks."

"Individual Racism is the type that is often conscious and intentional, and also personal, which is usually intended for one person or one specific group of people; like the blacks were subject to by the hands of the Europeans. For example, in the 1960's blacks were not allowed to ride in the front of the bus, or eat at restaurants with white people. Another example of segregation, within the human race, is when one group is separated from others by the policies of schools. White people didn't want their kids to attend the same schools as blacks.

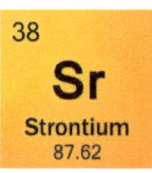

Words of His Imperial Majesty Haile Selassie I

"THE TRUE LEADER IS ONE WHO REALIZES BY FAITH THAT HE IS AN INSTRUMENT IN THE HANDS OF GOD, AND EDUCATES HIMSELF TO BE A GUIDE AND INSPIRER OF THE NOBLER SENTIMENTS AND ASPIRATIONS TO THE PEOPLE."

"The true leader that H.I.M. is speaking of, I think, is a leader who let's his own Ras (head) govern him through the power of providence. Therefore, everyone and everything he comes in contact with becomes and is used as a tool. And because he or she is propelled, and recognized that Jah The Almighty Himself is the divine conduit; by which all things work through for the highest elevation and inspiration, as he trod in this realm and in the realm of his head, he obtains the knowledge required to guide, inspirer, and motivate others; with excellent qualities and aptitude of superior mind and moral character."